I0698585

Management Guide for Businesses in 2024

The comprehensive tool to rank world class phenomenal (s). A push for Professionals, intermediate & beginners, in companies, firms and entrepreneurs, ready for a next level.

By

Francis A. Wiles

Copyright

Copyright 2023 Francis A. Wiles. Reserved rights apply. Without the publisher's prior written consent, no portion of this publication may be copied, distributed, or transmitted in any way, including by photocopying, recording, or other mechanical or electronic means, with the exception of brief quotations included in critical reviews and other non-commercial uses allowed by copyright law.

Disclaimer

The data in this "Management Guide for Businesses in 2024" is solely meant to be used for general informative purposes. The author and publisher do not make any express or implied claims or assurances on the availability, accuracy, suitability, completeness, or reliability of the information provided herein, despite having taken every precaution to ensure its accuracy and completeness. Any decisions made in reliance on the information in this guide, or for any errors or omissions in the content, are the sole responsibility of the author and publisher.

About the Author

Francis A. Wiles is an enthusiastic business coach and expert who is committed to enabling people and companies to experience extraordinary growth. Francis uses his extensive knowledge and awareness of the constantly changing business world to help his clients succeed by providing them with inspirational advice and strategic insights. Francis is well-known for his engaging coaching approach and for fusing his dedication to encouraging creativity and adaptability with real-world experience. Because of his unshakable faith in the potential of every company, he offers customized solutions that provide entrepreneurs the skills they need to overcome obstacles and turn their ideas into profitable businesses. The goal of Francis A. Wiles is to mentor and encourage people as they pursue business achievement

INTRODUCTION..**8**

Overview of the Current Business Landscape........11

Importance of Effective Management in 2024........14

CHAPTER 1: Emerging Trends in Business............17

Technology Integration..19

Strategies for effective technology integration........20

Sustainability Practices...25

Remote Work Dynamics...27

CHAPTER 2: Leadership Strategies........................31

Adaptive Leadership in a Changing Environment.. 49

Cultivating a Positive Work Culture........................ 53

CHAPTER 3: Digital Transformation........................83

Technologies for digital transformation.................. 86

The digital transformation process in six steps.......96

Digital transformation's future.............................. 103

CHAPTER 4: Strategic Planning............................ 105

Setting Clear Business Objectives........................109

The Significance of Well-Defined Objectives........ 111

Tips for Setting Effective Goals............................115

Risk Management Strategies................................121

Which are the essential risk management tools?. 128

Long-term Vision and Flexibility............................132

CHAPTER 5: Employee Engagement.................... 136

Motivating and Empowering Teams......................140

Effective Communication Strategies.....................144

Techniques for effective business communication145

Professional Development Programs...................158
CHAPTER 6: Customer-Centric Approach.............163
Why Does Customer Centricity Matter For
Companies And Brands?......................................166
Strategies for transforming into a Customer-Centric
business..170
Understanding Customer Needs.........................176
Building Lasting Customer Relationships.............179
Utilizing Feedback for Continuous Improvement..188
CHAPTER 7: Financial Management...................... 193
The Financial Management Goals........................195
Financial Management's Range........................... 196
Financial Management's Roles............................203
The Value of Sound Financial Management........209
Budgeting and Forecasting.................................215
Cost Optimization Strategies.............................. 221
CHAPTER 8: Crisis Management...........................226
Communication During Crises.............................231
Learning from Past Challenges...........................234
CHAPTER 9: Regulatory Compliance....................237
Staying Informed on Industry Regulations............241
Ethical Business Practices..................................245
Corporate Social Responsibility...........................248
CONCLUSION... 258
REVIEW PAGE...262

INTRODUCTION

Businesses will encounter many opportunities and problems in the changing business environment of 2024, which will call for skilled and visionary management. A thorough examination of the tactics required to successfully navigate the intricate workings of the modern business environment may be found in the Management Guide for Businesses in 2024.

Setting the scene, this introduction highlights the critical role successful management plays in attaining success while providing a succinct summary of the state of business today. As we explore this guide, readers will learn about new trends, disruptive technology, and changing expectations that are reshaping the business landscape.

This guide seeks to provide managers and leaders with the information and resources they need to flourish in the face of change in an era where adaptation is critical. This guide provides a compass for guiding organizations towards success in 2024 and beyond, whether it's utilizing technology, building a resilient organizational culture, or solving urgent global concerns.

Overview of the Current Business Landscape

Companies are situated at the nexus of extraordinary opportunities and hitherto unseen challenges. The contemporary corporate landscape is characterized by a swift inflow of technology innovations, a transformative global perspective towards sustainability, and a groundbreaking reinterpretation of work relationships. Businesses must reevaluate their plans, embrace innovation, and adjust to the shifting tides of customer expectations as we approach the dawn of a new age.

Technology is a powerful tool that is easily incorporated into all facets of business operations. Data analytics and artificial intelligence are not just catchphrases; they are essential instruments influencing how decisions are made. At the same time, sustainability has evolved beyond simple corporate social responsibility to become a distinguishing quality that customers actively look for in companies they do business with. The conventional office space has changed, and remote work is now an essential component of the contemporary workplace rather than merely a fad.

In the face of these revolutionary changes, companies struggle to survive and grow in this changing environment. In order to help leaders navigate this complex terrain, the "Management Guide for Businesses in 2024" seeks to serve as a compass. It provides insights and tactics for leading with resilience and foresight in this new era of business.

Importance of Effective Management in 2024

Effective management is extremely important and cannot be emphasized enough. The ability of enterprises to traverse previously unheard-of possibilities and problems has made management's position increasingly crucial to the success of the firm. A company's compass through the complexity of developing technologies, changing market conditions, and changing customer expectations is effective management.

In a time when survival and adaptability go hand in hand, competent management is the spark that ignites creativity and strategic advancement. A healthy organization is characterized by its capacity to lead teams with agility, cultivate a culture of resilience, and make well-informed decisions when faced with uncertainty. In 2024, effective management will go beyond operational effectiveness and require a strong dedication to the welfare of employees, moral behavior, and an ambitious plan that goes beyond short-term obstacles.

The "Management Guide for Businesses in 2024" acknowledges that management has a critical role in determining an organization's future. By providing leaders with this handbook, we hope to equip them with knowledge and tactics that will help them not only tackle today's problems but also set their companies up for long-term success in the rapidly evolving future.

CHAPTER 1: Emerging Trends in Business

Businesses are riding the tides of revolutionary changes that are redefining the basic structure of trade as we go toward 2024. The landscape is still being shaped by technology, which is a constant catalyst for change. From cutting-edge ideas to essential technologies that provide previously unheard-of efficiency and insights, artificial intelligence and data analytics have come a long way. Sustainability is becoming more and more of a customer expectation as well as a corporate duty, pushing companies to adopt environmentally friendly procedures.

Once a reaction to world events, remote work has evolved into a permanent fixture that is redefining the paradigm of the traditional office. Businesses are adopting flexible work arrangements as they see the advantages of having a distributed yet connected staff. Businesses are taking advantage of the growth of the metaverse in this era of increased connectivity by looking into new ways to interact and collaborate with their customers.

Technology Integration

In today's dynamic corporate environment, technology integration has become essential for organizations trying to stay afloat in the complex current market. The combination of advanced automation, data analytics, and artificial intelligence has moved beyond efficiency to become a key component of strategic decision-making.

Artificial intelligence enables businesses to extract valuable insights from large datasets through its ability to digest information quickly and recognize patterns. By transforming unstructured data into a strategic asset, data analytics offers a path forward for well-informed decision-making. Automation increases human capacities and streamlines repetitive processes, creating a synergistic effect that boosts production.

Companies must overcome the difficulty of not just implementing new technologies but also integrating them into day-to-day operations.

Strategies for effective technology integration

1. **Programmatic Strategy:** Create a well-defined technology integration plan that is in line with your corporate objectives. Determine the main areas where technology may improve overall operations, decision-making, and efficiency.

2. Investment in Training: Make sure the members of your team has the know-how to make use of emerging technology. Invest in training initiatives to empower staff members and promote an ongoing learning culture.

3. Interaction Across Functional Domains: Encourage communication and cooperation between IT professionals and other departments. The adoption of a cross-functional strategy guarantees that technological solutions are customized to address the unique requirements of different business units.

4. Flexibility and Scalability: Select technological solutions that are adaptable and scalable so they may change to meet your company's changing needs. This makes integration possible no matter how your business changes or expands.

5. User-Centric Design: When introducing new technology, give the user experience first priority. Employee adoption rates are increased by an intuitive design and user-friendly interface, which maximizes the benefits of the integrated technology.

6. Data Security Measures: To protect sensitive data, put strong cybersecurity measures in place. It becomes increasingly important to uphold the highest standards of data security as technological integration increases.

7. Pilot Programs: Before implementing new technologies widely, test them through pilot programs. This facilitates the detection and handling of possible problems, guaranteeing a more seamless integration procedure.

8. Ongoing Assessment and Development:

Evaluate integrated technology performance on a regular basis. To maximize efficiency, get user and stakeholder feedback and be ready to make changes or updates.

9. Conformity with Industry Guidelines:

Keep up with the latest needs for compliance and industry standards. Making sure that your technology integration complies with these guidelines reduces risks and improves your company's reputation.

10. Strategic Partnerships: Take into account collaborating with technology suppliers or specialists. Working together with outside

experts during the integration process might yield insightful information and helpful assistance.

Sustainability Practices

Sustainability has transformed from a corporate term to one of the most important guiding principles in today's business environment. In 2024, adopting sustainable practices will be a strategic requirement for enterprises rather than just a moral decision.

Using environmentally friendly practices throughout the supply chain is one important tactic. To reduce their negative environmental effects, firms are reassessing and streamlining many operations, from procuring raw materials to production and distribution. This not only fits in with what society expects, but it also puts businesses in a competitive position in a market where consumers are becoming more environmentally concerned.

The incorporation of renewable energy sources is another essential component. To lessen their carbon footprint, businesses are shifting to renewable energy sources like solar or wind power. This not only helps the global climate change effort, but it also frequently saves money in the long run.

Establishing a corporate responsibility culture is also essential. This entails encouraging waste reduction, assisting local communities, and including staff members in sustainability projects. These activities not only improve the company's image but also foster a healthy corporate culture that draws and keeps talent and customers.

Remote Work Dynamics

In the ever-changing field of work dynamics, remote work has become a distinguishing paradigm for the year 2024. A distributed workforce has replaced the traditional idea of a centralized workplace, changing how companies run and how people fulfill their professional obligations.

A crucial tactic for managing the dynamics of remote work is to make use of sophisticated collaborative technologies. Project management software, communication tools, and video conferencing allow team members to collaborate easily even when they are located in different places. Not only should in-person interactions be replicated, but a virtual environment that promotes productive communication and teamwork should also be established.

Redefining performance metrics is another essential component. The subtleties of remote work may not be adequately captured by conventional standards. Rather, companies are moving toward outcome-based evaluations, emphasizing output, output delivery, and the total effect of workers' efforts.

A difficult but crucial tactic is striking a balance between flexibility and structure. Schedules can be customized for each employee remotely, taking into account their preferences while maximizing output. Establishing precise rules and standards, however, makes sure that flexibility doesn't jeopardize the team's cohesiveness or the accomplishment of group objectives.

In remote work environments, the welfare of employees is paramount. Promoting a healthy work-life balance, encouraging frequent breaks, and addressing any feelings of isolation are some strategies. Businesses are making investments in programs that promote mental wellness and strengthen bonds between geographically dispersed personnel.

CHAPTER 2: Leadership Strategies

Leadership positions are crucial in all organizations because, in each given field, capable managers are required to guide their staff toward organizational goals. Senior leadership teams and managers can motivate staff by using effective leadership techniques. You can succeed in your management profession by becoming knowledgeable about various strategies. In this post, we define leadership techniques, provide instances of several approaches, and go over the benefits and drawbacks of each.

A company's leadership style is outlined in a leadership plan. It guarantees that an organization's leaders are working toward the same objectives. Even though your management style may be centered around a single leadership strategy, knowing the benefits of many methods will help you apply a range of techniques to your work. Various leadership styles are needed by different teams, departments, and workplaces; therefore, knowing the different kinds of leadership styles can be beneficial to your job.

Leadership techniques to raise the performance of your group

Effective managers have the power to change people's behavior and raise their team's output. Since different team members may respond differently to different methods, managers can better engage their teams by utilizing a variety of strategies. Among the tactics that managers can use are:

1. Develop your vision: Aspirational leaders must have a clear vision for the future of their group, division, or business. Anticipating the long-term success of your team can motivate team members to strive towards this future objective in addition to providing you with the motivation to perform effectively as a manager. The best goals are reachable, quantifiable, and well-defined so that you can explain your vision to others and make sure that the activities in your department are working toward a long-term goal. Consider the following benefits and drawbacks:

Pros:

- use long-term perspective

- establishes a broad departmental goal and offers a specific ambition for teams to work toward

Cons:

- Could promote idealism excessively
- Members might not agree with the vision; too much long-term planning could divert attention from immediate tasks.

2. Describe and express your vision: Developing, communicating, and outlining your vision for the group and division is one of the fundamental aspects of managing. To promote productivity and meaningful contribution, it is essential that each team member have a sense of commitment to a certain vision. To make sure that team members understand what is expected of them, effective managers clearly communicate their vision and make it relevant to the department. When it is feasible, they produce a workable road plan that aids the group in visualizing how to realize their goal. Think about these benefits and drawbacks:

Pros:

- aid in team members' comprehension of the goal

- divides the vision into manageable chunks and makes it relatable to every team member, fostering productive discussion and debate

Cons:

- Those on the team may have an impact on the vision if there is weak leadership.

- Those that disagree can see a decrease in output.

- For the department, a vision without a practical plan may seem unproductive.

3. Acknowledge the successes of others:

Enhancing team morale and motivating individuals to work as successfully as they can are achieved through the use of positive reinforcement. Acknowledging and thanking others for their accomplishments inspires them to keep up their current level of work.

A contented worker motivates others and devises innovative methods to enhance their output in order to receive further commendation. A workplace where rewards, recognition, and positivity are abundant fosters a desire to work. Examine these benefits and drawbacks of acknowledging others' accomplishments:

Pros:

- Positive reinforcement motivates team members to provide recognition affirms a worker's efforts and gives team members a sense of value

Cons:

- Praise that is improperly given could breed favoritism.

- When someone on the team receives recognition, other teammates could respond negatively.

- Some people may make up their contributions in order to get credit.

4. Promote two-way dialogue: In a professional setting, comments from managers can help employees grow personally and learn from their mistakes. Communication is essential. It's easy for managers to forget that receiving feedback from their team can help them become better leaders because they assign assignments, offer criticism and appreciation, and provide the framework for team members to contribute successfully.

Departments are able to operate more honestly and exchange ideas more effectively when they communicate in both directions. As a result, everyone feels heard and a spirit of camaraderie is fostered. Consider the following benefits and drawbacks:

Pros:

- Two-way communication fosters an honest and open work environment, helps managers feel like they are being led with integrity, and makes team members feel respected.

Cons:

- Possibility of managers or staff being insulted by critical feedback

- A lively and distracting environment could result from communication, and some team members might not enjoy talking to each other at work.

5. Uphold honesty: Important duties of a manager include upholding honesty, inspiring a team to align with the organization's beliefs and values, and creating a positive work environment. The manager becomes an inspiration to the workforce when they regard them as the cornerstone around which they should build their own conduct, work ethic, and output. The manager must live up to the organization's ideals and uphold them under all conditions in order for the department to remain morally pure. Among the benefits and drawbacks are:

Pros:

- Ensuring that all team members are aware of the organization's values and instills them in a department.

- creates a base from which staff members may work

Cons:

- Ignorant bosses could uphold false values

- Some supervisors might treat staff members harshly.

- The group might not pay attention to the leader.

6. Set a good example: By definition, leaders model behavior, contributions, and methods of operation for those under their direction. A manager may come seem as weak or inexperienced to their staff if they lack extensive practical experience or a solid understanding of strategies. Some leaders may use a knowledge-forward strategy in order to leverage their expertise and experience to benefit their team. Others would prefer a man-management approach to leadership, which is setting an example and using people skills to motivate people to do their best. A few benefits and drawbacks could be:

Pros:

- Teach the team how to work together by using their interpersonal and practical experience to grow personnel. This enables the team members to look up to the management as an inspiration.

Cons:

- Inexperienced or ignorant managers may find it difficult to motivate team members; leaders with poor interpersonal skills may set a poor example for others.

7. Assign and empower your group:

Appropriate task delegation by good leaders empowers their team members and builds on each person's strengths. Knowing each worker's advantages and disadvantages enables the manager to determine who would be most effective on a given task. When workers are involved in a task they are comfortable with, the overall quality of the work is higher. When deciding whether to empower and delegate to your team, weigh the following benefits and drawbacks:

Pros:

- Workers put in greater effort on assignments they are comfortable with; managers know exactly who is responsible for what; and when everyone works hard and contributes well, the team feels empowered.

Cons:

- Managers could assign tasks improperly.

- A disconnected work dynamic is caused by a lack of understanding of employees, and certain team members may desire greater control over their work.

8. Promote expansion and advancement:

A competent leader fosters growth and development so that followers can realize their greatest potential. It is the delight of professional development for many team members, and it is the responsibility of a leader to foster that development. When workers perceive a noticeable progress, they believe they are adding value to the company, which fosters a more advantageous working environment for both parties. Consider the following benefits and drawbacks:

Pros:

fosters a positive work atmosphere

encourages workers to advance in their careers

Organizations gain from higher production quality.

Cons:

Members of the team could depart from the company.

Some people could feel abandoned.

A superiority complex may emerge among some team members.

9. Strive for ongoing education: Learning is a constant that helps people grow and accomplish their goals no matter how far they travel in life. Leaders in their departments push for ongoing education so that employees can advance in their professions. This creates a good habit of being open to learning regardless of the situation. Think about these benefits and drawbacks:

Pros:

- Can learn in any circumstance.

- Gaining knowledge results in the growth of abilities.

- Workers can improve the caliber of their work.

Cons:

- People could decide to study irrelevant subjects.

- There's a chance that some people will sense information overload.

- Workers might not desire to participate in additional training.

10. Be confident rather than combative: Every leader has moments when they need to be forceful, but some may go too far and act aggressively. Aggression and assertiveness are clearly different; the former uses constructive methods to discipline, while the latter unnecessarily lowers morale. When needed, effective leaders gently and using language that promotes positivity and support will gently but firmly push team members. Consider the following benefits and drawbacks:

Pros:

- demonstrates great leadership abilities; constructively disciplines staff; establishes a clear hierarchy of respect.

Cons:

- Some may not recognize the differences; anger fosters a hostile environment; aggressive behavior may destroy professional relationships.

Adaptive Leadership in a Changing Environment

Flexible leadership is essential for the success of any enterprise. Adaptive leadership, in contrast to traditional leadership approaches, acknowledges that change is inevitable and calls for a flexible, adaptable strategy.

Adaptive leaders foster a culture of ongoing learning among their teams by embracing a keen awareness of the changing environment. They are skilled at handling ambiguity and can make defensible choices even when all the facts aren't known. This entails anticipating and proactively directing change rather than merely responding to it.

One essential quality of adaptable leaders is flexibility. They are aware that inflexible procedures and hierarchies can hinder creativity. Rather, they cultivate an atmosphere that promotes innovation and views failure as a necessary step toward advancement. This calls for a readiness to reevaluate tactics, change course when needed, and foster perseverance in the face of failures.

A key component of adaptive leadership is communication. A compelling vision must be communicated by leaders, who must also be open about difficulties and changes. Team members' trust is strengthened by this open communication, which also helps everyone comprehend the organization's objectives.

Cultivating a Positive Work Culture

Employees are guided by work culture when it comes to what actions, standards, and issues are essential to the company's current mission. It also develops and changes as conditions change.

An organization's values, beliefs, and attitudes are all part of its work culture. It establishes standards for how staff members ought to act and communicate with one another as they carry out their daily duties and support the overarching goal of the business. Within a business, there are also smaller work cultures, such as those in management, engineering, and employee relations.

A company's essential principles are not the same as its work culture; they change with time.

Its unwavering commitment to the consumer, its high regard for innovation, and its firm conviction that everything is possible when working together will never waver.

Why Does Workplace Culture Matter?

Job happiness, workplace engagement, and individual and team morale are just a few of the important aspects of the employee experience that can be significantly impacted by work culture. As per the Society for Human Resource Management report, 94 percent of managers believe that "a positive workplace culture creates a resilient team of employees."

It is challenging to recruit and retain talented staff when a firm adopts practices that negatively affect workplace culture and foster a toxic team dynamic. According to a 2022 poll of job searchers, "company values and culture" was cited by 23% of participants as having the biggest impact on their decision to accept a job offer. According to the same poll, 34% of job searchers left their job within the first 90 days because the "company culture was not as expected," and 21% cited "poor company culture" as their main reason for quitting in the previous year.

Every corporation will inevitably develop a work culture, sometimes to the disadvantage of the company. An unpleasant and costly work experience will result from allowing undesirable behaviors and toxic attitudes to fester. A survey by the Society for Human Resource Management states that during a five-year period, toxic workplace environments cost U.S. firms $223 billion in attrition.

company culture influences consumers' decision to do business with you as well as employees in the company. For instance, customers use social media platforms beyond just reading employee feedback about a business. In their talks with sales teams, they are also asking direct questions. Potential clients will pose queries in the request for bids (RFP). We'll be asked to explain our culture to them. Thus, it has featured in some of the sales processes of the clients, according to Herrera.

Workplace Culture Components

Workplace culture is shaped by a number of things. Based on data from Glassdoor, research by the MIT Sloan School of Management and CultureX determined the top ten cultural components that matter to employees:

- having a sense of respect.
- possessing a leadership that is encouraging.
- if a leader's actions are consistent with their principles.
- supervisors who encourage a poisonous work atmosphere.
- seeing unethical activity.
- advantages.
- Benefits and facilities.

- Possibilities for education and career advancement.
- Job security.
- Both the number and caliber of reorganizations.

The steps that a company takes to influence team culture, whether positively or negatively, can have a big impact on how fulfilled their employees feel. Individuals who are not satisfied with their jobs are less inclined to work hard to help the company succeed or to refer others to their current employer.

According to a 2022 Quantum Workplace poll, employees say they are most affected by their employers' performance management, celebrations, and recognition policies, as well as their corporate vision and values. Ensuring that employees feel their opinions are heard and their individual contributions are valued is one of these fundamental components of work culture.

When describing their ideal workplace cultures, survey participants frequently used adjectives like flexible, inclusive, pleasant, collaborative, and enjoyable. According to the majority of workers, managers and leaders are the first to define and communicate culture. However, more than half also believe that each employee, regardless of rank, plays a unique role in establishing culture.

How to Establish a Happy Work Environment

Identify your key principles before you begin creating the work culture you envision for your organization. These ought to serve as the cornerstone of everything that occurs at your business and direct the development of your enterprise.

All key stakeholders should be included, so set aside as much time as needed to make sure everyone is on the same page. This should include leadership, long-term workers, and HR reps. Ultimately, you have to have a succinct set of values that precisely captures the culture of your business now and your long-term objectives.

Next, consider the kind of workplace culture you wish to establish. Take into account everything, including the office's physical design and the frequency with which staff members communicate with managers, C-Suite members, and coworkers. The actual job starts there.

How to Enhance Culture at Work

Workplace culture improvement takes time. Long-term, sustainable change requires dedication, and it begins at the top of the organizational hierarchy. It needs leaders who are prepared to lead by example in terms of regular communication, responsibility, and openness.

Leaders who are trying to change the culture of the company must be prepared to invest in the projects that their team members care about the most. According to a survey, offering "professional development opportunities" ranked highest among suggestions for enhancing workplace culture. According to a different survey, 38% of job applicants would decline an offer from an organization that didn't have a strategy in place to promote diversity or that didn't have a diverse workforce.

Most respondents claim to be able to determine whether they would mesh well with a company's culture in less than a month, and many even claim to be able to do so in less than a week. It is vital that businesses begin implementing significant cultural transformation as soon as possible.

Tips for Enhanced workplace culture

- Establish definite goals to direct staff performance.
- Long term objectives are essential to be recognized by the workers.
- Launch diversity campaigns and encourage inclusive behavior.

- Promote openness and transparency in departmental and managerial communications as well as team member interactions.

- Give each employee a seat at the table and give them the freedom to express their opinions.

- To build enduring relationships, provide staff members the chance to get to know one another both inside and outside of the workplace.

Extra Tips

Identify Particular Goals: Describe each team's goals so that workers have specific targets to strive toward. This will not only support teamwork among members but also aid direct individual performance. As needed, make sure there is space for feedback to modify KPIs and quotas. For instance, you may wish to adjust a team's target goals to increase output if they are consistently meeting their goals without exerting much effort.

Publish the goals of the Organization: Aside from departmental goals, ensure that all staff members understand the organization's long-term aims. People will be able to develop a feeling of purpose in their work because of this. A source of incentive that goes beyond quarterly targets will show how important each position is to accomplishing the goal of the business.

Ensure inclusivity and diversity: Foster a friendly and inclusive work environment by embracing the diversity of individuals and appreciating their individuality. Encourage staff members to use inclusive language by sharing their pronouns with the team, and think about forming a committee to support diversity initiatives. As your company expands, make sure diversity and inclusion remain key components by collaborating with the HR department to incorporate diversity into your recruitment strategy.

Permit for levity of spirit

There are stressful times at work, and being able to lighten a tense environment is a crucial ability. Of course, solving the issue should be the ultimate aim, but doing so with a positive attitude and new eyes is more fruitful than doing otherwise. People seldom succeed unless they are enjoying what they are doing, as American writer and lecturer Dale Carnegie once stated. If you can afford to look on the bright side and reassure your staff that you have their back, they will repay the favor by working even harder.

Set respect as priority: All employees should have a sense of worth and inclusion, irrespective of their position within the organization. Compared to delegating for hectic work, internships offer a far bigger advantage, and new hires provide a different viewpoint. Every employee should feel empowered to express their ideas and have a seat at the table since you never know where the next amazing idea may come from.

Set up a touch zero tolerance guidance: Ensuring that workers understand their rights and individuality are protected at work is equally as vital as fostering a friendly workplace. Giving staff members the freedom to freely discuss problems they are having both within and outside of the workplace and the means to get the assistance and resources they require is a critical component of a supportive work environment. Make sure HR staff members can adjust their schedules to accommodate private meetings when necessary. You should also think about setting up an anonymous hotline for employees to report occurrences of sexual harassment in the workplace, which would provide a safe and discreet means for them to do so.

Set up a program for employee recognition: Employees should be honored for their exceptional work. By doing this, you may motivate staff members to keep up their outstanding work and give them a sense of importance in the organization. Additionally, it will inspire their colleagues to perform better, creating a culture of healthy rivalry at work that promotes excellence.

Accept and use the feedback from your employee: Try shifting your viewpoint on feedback, in fact. Instead of viewing it as a sign that anything is amiss, examine the possibility that your staff is attempting to improve the company because they genuinely care about it and its success. Instead of letting their problems fester and ultimately quitting the firm out of frustration, they are choosing to bring their pain spots to your attention, which offers you the chance to fix them.

Remember to be adaptable: Things will arise in life and get in the way. Workers shouldn't worry about consequences if they take time off to handle personal obligations or other issues. For instance, if a worker is having trouble juggling work and family obligations, attempt to come to an agreement that would enable them to contribute effectively at work without compromising their personal lives. Rather than being known for being inflexible and distant, you'll get the admiration of your staff. Furthermore, offering flexible schedules can help you draw in top talent. According to nearly 50% of job searchers, a company should provide them with "flexibility and autonomy."

Change with the times: Employees that are fully invested in the company's success are deserving of the trust of your leadership group. Encourage openness and honesty in communication between team members, management, and department heads. By doing this, a pleasant work environment where people feel appreciated and heard will be created. To provide the team with important information, think about starting a recurring internal newsletter. You could also have a monthly town hall meeting to discuss company-wide events that need further explanation.

Organize social events: People are sociable creatures who long for connection. To encourage deep relationships amongst employees, provide them the chance to get to know one another both inside and outside of the workplace. Organizing a hybrid Friday happy hour at the office and providing online access for remote workers is a simple way to keep things simple. When brainstorming new ideas for your work culture, consider what kinds of activities your team would most enjoy.

Don'ts in Work Culture

Never improve workers to work through launch: Even though it's not legally necessary, letting workers turn off their computers for 30 to 60 minutes per day fosters a healthy work environment. It is impractical and harmful to expect your team members to produce high-quality work nonstop for eight hours without a break, as they are not machines. Furthermore, it implies that workers are not regarded as persons but rather solely for the output of their employment. It has been demonstrated that taking regular breaks increases productivity, and 81 percent of workers who take a daily lunch break say they would like to be more actively involved in their company.

Not changing schedules for one -on-one: Try your best to keep your appointment if you have scheduled a one-on-one meeting with an employee, even if something else comes up. By doing this, you'll demonstrate that you appreciate and value their time as well as your interest in what they have to say.

Avoid making it simple for disengaged employees to return: Employee disengagement will impede growth, whereas an engaged staff can help your business move forward on its path to success. Pull people aside to have a conversation about their conduct if you see them doing things that are detrimental to the success of your team. It's time to split ways and assist them in finding a different role that better fits their needs and objectives if, despite your best efforts, nothing changes. Disengaged workers occasionally need a little help to get back on their feet when they're in a rut in their careers.

Never limit your opportunities for learning by job descriptions: Developing one's skills is crucial to having a fulfilling work experience. Permit workers to follow their interests both within and beyond the workplace, and promote information exchange among coworkers. Collaboration, camaraderie, and employee connections will all increase as a result of this knowledge sharing.

Avoid hirement based work on work culture fit: Hiring for cultural additions rather than cultural fits is a crucial component of fostering a varied workplace community. Finding applicants that offer a distinct viewpoint and who share and live your fundamental values is the goal of the cultural ad recruiting model. Seek people who will benefit your team rather than just fit in, as you want to grow and enhance both your company and work culture.

Never set up with awful managers: Employee performance and engagement are directly impacted by managers. Nearly 90% of workers say that their manager "contributes to setting their work team environment." Managers interact with their direct reports the most, so it's important to make sure those who are leading a team are doing so with conviction and in line with your core values. In fact, 81 percent of workers who consider their work culture to be "poor" have witnessed a manager allow others in the workplace "to get away with bad behavior."

Ask not to assumption HR to do everything:

Despite HR teams' best efforts, a small group of people do not build an organization's culture. HR teams cannot be expected to handle this duty alone; it requires a collective effort. When people collaborate, cultures that are positive are formed.

Avoid forcing it: Workplace environments that are rewarding and positive don't happen by accident. It will develop naturally if you stick to your principles, pay attention to your staff, and enjoy yourself. Workplace cultures that support employee happiness and company growth are worth the time investment. Success in a business depends on fostering a healthy work environment where everyone is appreciated, valued, and feels at home. Make sure you consider the input provided by your staff and rely on them to assist in creating a positive work environment.

Diversity and Inclusion Initiatives

Diversity and Inclusion (D&I) initiatives have evolved from being ethical imperatives to strategic advantages for businesses. Recognizing the inherent value of diverse perspectives, successful organizations are actively cultivating inclusive environments that go beyond mere representation.

Initiating diversity starts with recruitment strategies that prioritize inclusivity. Companies are actively seeking talent from varied backgrounds, ensuring a rich tapestry of experiences and ideas. Moreover, fostering an inclusive workplace extends beyond hiring, encompassing ongoing efforts to provide equal opportunities for professional development and career advancement.

Leadership commitment is integral to the success of D&I initiatives. Top-down advocacy reinforces the importance of diversity, setting the tone for inclusive policies and practices. Transparent communication and accountability mechanisms ensure that diversity is not just a box to tick but an ingrained part of the organizational culture.

Employee resource groups and mentorship programs are becoming commonplace, providing platforms for underrepresented individuals to connect, share experiences, and receive guidance. Training programs on unconscious bias and cultural competence further contribute to creating a workplace where everyone feels valued and heard.

CHAPTER 3: Digital Transformation

Digital Transformation: What Is It?

Digitization and digital transformation are two related ideas that are sometimes confused with one another. The most basic of these is digitization, which is the conversion of analog or manual information into digital form. An example of this would be the conversion of handwritten records into computerized records. The process of employing digital technology and capabilities to perform many of the tasks you perform on a daily basis in new and improved ways that produce better results is known as digitalization.

Digital transformation starts with digitalization. Furthermore, you can rethink how you employ people, technology, and processes to advance your organization in new directions thanks to digital transformation.

In the modern corporate world, "digital transformation" refers to the process of switching from analog and manual to digital processes in all areas of the company, such as operations, customer service, supply chain, and ERP. In essence, digital transformation connects people, places, and things to enable organizations and other entities to produce better outcomes. Every business is transforming digitally for a different reason. Some may be motivated by chances for expansion or heightened competition, while others may be motivated by shifting regulatory requirements.

For whatever reason a business chooses to go down this route, the end product may be improved products, experiences, and services that either match or surpass the expectations of the client. Enhanced innovation and profitability can be achieved through improved efficiencies and other business benefits. The goal of digital transformation in the public sector is to improve citizen quality of life while simultaneously conserving resources.

Technologies for digital transformation

Applications and software, networking capabilities, artificial intelligence (AI), machine learning, augmented and virtual reality, the Internet of Things (IoT), sensing technology, video-based analytics, cloud computing, and other technologies are all included under the broad heading of digital transformation. When it comes to digital transformation, it's crucial to keep in mind that selecting the appropriate technology to accomplish your goals is more important than selecting a particular one.

Digital transformation history

The earliest computers, which converted handwritten notes into computational data that could be processed, analyzed, and shared, marked the beginning of the lengthy history of digital transformation. These capabilities developed along with the introduction of networking and the internet, and datasets became incredibly enormous. Large data necessitated more reliable digital data analysis and management procedures, which were backed by data lakes, data centers, and data warehouses.

The need for ever-increasing capabilities to manage, analyze, and process the huge volumes of data that are being generated led to the development of the cloud. Since then, advances in IoT, AI, and machine learning have made even more advanced technological choices available to businesses looking to transform their operations and improve results. Virtual and augmented reality, as well as technologies based on video analytics, are among the cutting-edge capabilities that are facilitating the broad digital revolution.

Three essential components of digital transformation

There is much more to digital transformation than just installing new hardware. It necessitates a calculated strategy that takes care of three fundamental components.

1 Material: In the sense that it uses technology to move the company from manual to digital operations, digital transformation is physical. Examples of physical transformation include the switch from paper-based recordkeeping to electronic data collecting; the application of robotics, artificial intelligence, and machine learning; and the installation of data sensors that convey information.

2 Mental: Cognitive digital transformation is made possible by digitalization, which includes AI and machine learning. This allows for sophisticated data analysis to be performed by machines, mimicking human thought processes. The demand for expert-level knowledge workers is being driven by these capabilities, which are also transforming the jobs of data scientists and analysts.

3.Cultural:

Because it involves people who are accustomed to behaving and responding in particular ways in their surroundings, such as at work or home, digital transformation is cultural. In the digital age, employees collaborate with "smart" machines. Employee roles adapt to new technology-enabled capabilities and procedures. A solid foundation for success may be established by making sure that everyone is aware of the need of transformation and has the tools necessary to bring about the change.

The advantages of the digital shift

Digitally driven operational improvements that generate more value for partners, employees, and customers can help almost any firm in any market. The following are some advantages that digital transformation can bring about:

- deeper, actionable insights based on analytics
- quicker and more effective procedures
- Enhanced capability
- Lower expenses
- increased productivity, quality, and safety

The chance to combine next-generation automation with business process improvement can meet evolving expectations and yield more value. Instead of concentrating on lead generation, successful companies now prioritize relationship selling, streamlining the purchasing process to avoid drawn-out discussions over terms and conditions, and fostering collaborative success by managing technology on behalf of clients rather than granting licenses for clients to use and integrate on their own to achieve their own goals.

Illustrations of the digital age

Here are a few instances of how digital transformation improves outcomes for various entities and industries:

Producing: By enabling predictive maintenance and process enhancements that lower downtime and scrap while guaranteeing the production of high-quality items, IoT may increase manufacturing efficiency and profitability. Without even needing to purchase a plane ticket, augmented reality systems may bring experts from abroad straight into the factory and offer better, less expensive training.

Shop: Digitalization in retail uses platforms, channels, and devices to offer seamless consumer experiences that are customized to meet individual customer needs. Retailers are using chatbots, artificial intelligence (AI), and advanced data analytics to create and offer tailored recommendations that effectively appeal to a single audience. The in-store experience is also changing as a result of digitalization, with more convenient customer service procedures and an interesting interactive setting.

Medical Care: In order to produce patient-centric and value-based results that benefit patients, providers, and payers while also cutting costs, the healthcare sector is utilizing a range of digital capabilities. Networked electronic medical records and virtual doctor consultations are only two examples of how digitization is changing the healthcare industry.

Digitally enabled "smart cities" are becoming more efficient while offering their residents a safer and higher quality of life. These cities combine state-of-the-art digital technologies with pre-existing physical infrastructures. Technologies like sensors, artificial intelligence, and video analytics are assisting the public sector in changing the way it delivers key services to achieve greater efficiency, reduced costs, and a higher level of citizen engagement. These services range from utility monitoring to public safety to environmental sustainability.

The digital transformation process in six steps

When you're ready to start a digital transformation, there are a lot of things to think about. A strong strategic strategy is necessary for success. Customers and staff will gain when procedures are streamlined and made simpler with the correct plan in place. You may enable them to finish jobs on their own, delight them with satisfying experiences, and automate as much as you can to relieve them of work. The actions listed below can assist you in creating such a plan:

1. Describe your online goals: The first step is exploration, when you decide why you want to change and what your goals are. This is the cornerstone that will guide the remainder of your actions.

2. Chart your online course: Whether your goal is to improve customer satisfaction or revolutionize industrial operations, you need to have a clear idea of how digitalization fits into your workflow and how it will help you reach your goals.

3. Assess your level of digital maturity: You may determine how far along your company has come in utilizing digital capabilities and where you still need to make improvements in terms of technology and procedures by conducting a digital maturity assessment. You can also determine the pace of your transformation with the aid of this examination.

4. Examine your digital skills: In order to select technology that bridges any existing gaps in your digital infrastructure, this is the time to discover such gaps. Creating a model that unifies people, data, processes, and tools on a single, integrated platform will allow you to execute toward objectives quickly and nimbly.

5. Create a roadmap for your transition: The groundwork for a transformational road plan is laid by steps 1 through This roadmap should outline the architecture required to optimize value and minimize risk and expense for any transformational projects you may be working on. It should also be clear and actionable. Additionally, it needs to be flexible enough to adjust to shifting priorities and newly developed technologies.

6. Cloud apps can help you achieve digital vision more quickly: Use cloud apps with future-ready, integrated, end-to-end business processes that define entire transformative processes for you and help you accelerate business growth to help you outpace change.

The stars of the digital revolution; their secrets

The foundation of a successful digital transformation is a thorough comprehension of user and customer needs. What needs to be changed and how are determined by this understanding. To be sure you're making the appropriate adjustments to fulfill those demands, pay attention to some advice from people who have completed the journey successfully. Ask for opinions from your staff and clients. The only way to know how to address the requirements of your consumers and staff is to engage with them continuously.

Define the problems that need to be solved based on the feedback. You can determine what has to be changed after you are aware of what your staff and consumers expect.

Create a plan that turns challenges into extraordinary opportunities. Create a plan that simplifies your experiences, gives your clients and staff more authority, and makes a difference in the lives of people you serve after you've recognized your difficulties.

Utilize cloud computing to adapt to the shifting demands and desires of both clients and staff. Seek for technology that helps you keep up with change while also allowing you to completely rethink your company. You can take advantage of cutting-edge technology as it is developed and remain ahead of customer and employee needs using cloud computing.

What unites the stars of the digital transition

At the end of the day, four factors determine whether you reach your goals:

- a strong, dependable, and continuous CEO transformation mandate.

- a cohesive, unwavering emphasis on the organizational goal that takes the place of a siloed mentality.

- A relentless sense of need that propels change at a faster rate.

- executive stewardship provided by a top leader with vision who is not bound to a particular industry or role.

Digital transformation's future

People's work, leisure, and daily lives are being transformed by digital transformation, and there is no sign that this revolutionary process is slowing down. Advances in digital technology consistently present chances for companies to add value for clients and enhance people's lives. New technologies that can help achieve revolutionary goals will surely keep coming up in the future.

Your success will depend on how well you implement a digital transformation that targets current business difficulties and addresses strategic objectives. To stay competitive and provide better services to its consumers, digitalization is eventually going to have to become a strategic cornerstone for every business and organization.

The most crucial thing to keep in mind during this endeavor is that the strength of digital transformation arises from first determining your use cases, and then selecting the technology, strategy, and collaborators that can turn those use cases into smooth, linked experiences that advance your company.

CHAPTER 4: Strategic Planning

In 2024, strategic planning will serve as a compass to help firms navigate the ever-changing landscape of possibilities and obstacles. It's a dynamic process that synchronizes organizational objectives with changing market conditions, guaranteeing resilience and sustainable growth, rather than just a bureaucratic exercise.

Delicately defining business objectives is essential to strategic planning. This entails a thorough examination of customer behavior, market developments, and competitive environments. Businesses can set attainable objectives that align with their distinct strengths and beliefs by comprehending the external factors at work.

One essential component of strategic planning is risk management. Businesses need to be aware of the uncertainties in the world and plan ahead by creating proactive risk mitigation plans. In order to make sure that companies are ready to handle a variety of future paths, scenario planning is required.

A forward-thinking perspective is also necessary for strategic planning. Businesses need to develop a long-term vision that accounts for changes in the market and developments in technology, in addition to short-term objectives. This entails welcoming innovation and maintaining adaptability in the face of sudden changes.

One of the most important tactics in successful strategic planning is cross-functional cooperation. Incorporating varied viewpoints from several divisions guarantees a comprehensive comprehension of obstacles and prospects. This cooperative strategy encourages creativity and increases the probability of effective execution.

In order to make real-time strategy adjustments, key performance indicators (KPIs) must be tracked and evaluated. Frequent evaluations enable companies to take advantage of new opportunities and adjust to changing conditions.

Setting Clear Business Objectives

Setting specific business goals is more than simply a routine task in the dynamic landscape of 2024; it's a strategic need that determines an organization's course. Having well-defined goals helps to steer teams, resources, and activities in the direction of a shared goal. We'll examine the significance of establishing specific company goals, practical goal-setting techniques, and real-world case studies that highlight the transformational potential of a well-defined purpose in this in-depth investigation.

The Significance of Well-Defined Objectives

Organizations can benefit from having clear business objectives because they provide them a sense of direction in an uncertain environment. They act as the cornerstone around which decisions and strategies are constructed. Essentially, well stated goals serve as a uniting factor, bringing all the many aspects of a company together to work toward shared aims. Setting specific goals for your organization is crucial for the following reasons:

1. Effort Alignment: Having clearly defined objectives guarantees that all members of the organization are aware of the main aims. In order to create a cohesive and cooperative work atmosphere where each team member meaningfully contributes toward shared objectives, this alignment is essential.

2. Attention and Ordering:

Businesses can efficiently allocate resources and prioritize projects when they have well-defined objectives. This emphasis makes it easier to stay focused and guarantees that efforts and resources are allocated to projects that directly advance predetermined objectives.

3. Performance Measurement: Clearly stated goals offer a quantifiable benchmark by which accomplishments can be evaluated. This helps identify areas that could need correction or enhancement in addition to allowing organizations to monitor their progress.

4. Incentives and Involvement: When workers comprehend the significance of their task and how it advances larger company objectives, they become more driven. Having defined goals gives team members a feeling of direction and encourages motivation and participation.

5. Flexibility:A decision-making reference point in a company environment that is changing quickly is provided by well-defined objectives. Having clearly stated objectives enables businesses to modify their tactics without losing sight of their ultimate goal when unanticipated difficulties develop.

Tips for Setting Effective Goals

Establishing specific goals for your company calls for careful planning and strategic thinking. The following are crucial tactics to guarantee that goal-setting procedures are successful:

1. SMART Criteria: Time-bound, Relevant, Specific, Measurable, and Achievable objectives are required (SMART). This framework makes ensuring that objectives are precise, measurable, reasonable, connected to more general goals, and have a fixed timeframe for fulfillment.

2. Incorporate Stakeholder Input: Take into account feedback from a range of stakeholders, including as staff members, clients, and investors. Engaging a range of viewpoints guarantees that goals are all-encompassing, aligned with the organization's principles, and capable of meeting external demands.

3. Continuous Evaluation and Modifications:
Because business environments are dynamic, goals must be reviewed and adjusted on a regular basis. Organizations are better equipped to handle unforeseen obstacles, grasp new possibilities, and adjust to changing conditions when regular assessments are conducted.

4. Transparency and Communication:
Effective communication is essential. Make sure that the organization as a whole is aware of the goals and is communicating them openly. This encourages comprehension, buy-in, and a group commitment to accomplishing common objectives.

Practical life Instances:

1. Google - Our Vision is to Organize All Information Worldwide:

Google's mission statement states that the company's main goal is to organize the world's knowledge and make it widely useful and accessible. The company's innovation in search algorithms, cloud services, and other information-related technologies has been driven by this specific and audacious ambition.

2. Tesla: Quickening the Global Shift to Renewable Energy:

The goal of Tesla's mission is to hasten the global switch to sustainable energy. This goal has propelled Tesla's concentration on energy storage technologies, solar energy solutions, and electric cars, establishing the business as a pioneer in the field of sustainable technology.

3. Amazon: The Company That Values Customers the Most on Earth:

Being the most customer-focused corporation on Earth is Amazon's main goal. Amazon has become a worldwide e-commerce behemoth thanks to its unwavering dedication to ease, quick delivery, and a wide range of goods and services. This customer-focused purpose has guided its efforts.

4. SpaceX - Creating Interplanetary Life:

Elon Musk established SpaceX with the bold goal of enabling interplanetary life. The company's attempts to create reusable rocket technology, reduce space travel costs, and eventually make it possible to colonize other planets have been guided by this ambition.

Well-defined goals have a transformational potential that goes beyond simple tasks; they inspire teams, change organizational culture, and put companies in a position to prosper in the face of uncertainty. Empirical evidence suggests that companies with well-defined goals and objectives not only successfully traverse the complex business environment of today, but also have a significant impact on the future direction of their respective industries.

Risk Management Strategies

I like to say there are 6 fundamental risk management techniques:

1. **Avoidance:** Although it is frequently impossible to totally avoid risk, it is nonetheless important to consider the possibilities. To reduce the risk of auto accidents during bad weather, Physical Plant, for instance, may decide not to release vehicles for travel until the weather starts to clear. On campus, water issues have repeatedly arisen in some buildings. It may be possible to prevent some water damage claims by forbidding the storage of documents or supplies in specific locations.

2. **Retention**: In certain cases, even though there are alternative ways to manage the risk, keeping the risk or a portion of it may be more economical depending on the likelihood and seriousness of the hazards that are being presented. For instance, because it is challenging to list and assess every kind of structure, the University is still at risk of damage from fences, signs, gates, and light poles. With the exception of circumstances when a third party's carelessness is involved, losses are covered by the campus maintenance budget. The majority of university personal property is still at risk of loss, even with insurance.

3. **Spreading**: The risk of damage to people and property can be dispersed. Spreading

risk can be exemplified by making duplicate copies of records and papers and keeping them in separate locations. The whole set of operational records for a department can be destroyed by a little fire in one room. Spreading out the danger of possible fatalities or serious injuries can be achieved by housing individuals in several buildings as opposed to a single facility.

4. **Loss Prevention and Reduction:** The frequency and severity of losses can frequently be reduced when there is no way to prevent the risk. To lower the chance of theft, risk management, for instance, promotes the installation of security mechanisms on specific audiovisual equipment. Students who are

studying abroad are required by the university to acquire health insurance in order to protect themselves from the possibility of financial hardship in the event that they need medical attention overseas.

5. **Transfer:** Risk may occasionally be passed on to other parties, usually through a contract. The risk of the event is transferred from the University to the facility user when outside groups utilize University facilities for public events. They are required to show proof of insurance and list the University as an extra insured under their policy. Since the policy essentially transfers the financial risk of loss from the covered entity to the insurance firm under contract, buying

insurance is also known as risk transfer. Insurance ought to be the very last resort, applied only after every other strategy has been tried and tested.

6. **Contracts:** Frequently, suppliers and service providers will try to absolve themselves of all responsibility for whatever conduct they take in connection with the deal by using a contract. These are commonly known as indemnity or "hold harmless" provisions. The President has given staff in Contracts & Procurement exclusive authority to make contracts on behalf of the University due to the difficulty in interpreting these rules. In response to requests from Contracts & Procurement, the Office of University Risk Management examines contracts and

agreements to evaluate insurance standards, identify and analyze risks, and review hold harmless and indemnity clauses. In most cases, the Chancellor's Office demands that the University get both an endorsement and a certificate of insurance. The part of the contracting procedure that takes the longest to complete is frequently gathering these documents.

Which are the essential risk management tools?

All department and unit plans and activities should incorporate risk identification and assessment during the planning and development phase. Take the following actions to evaluate the risks associated with a program or activity:

List the tasks related to the activity or program. For instance, going to an off-site location, getting ready for the experiment, carrying it out, cleaning it up, and getting rid of any trash are all possible tasks involved in carrying out a lab experiment. Determine the risks connected to each task. It is crucial to thoroughly identify the duties involved and the risks they pose. Unidentified risks cannot be controlled! For instance, inadequate setup and a lack of necessary equipment could be preparation-related dangers for the experiment. Analyze and decide on risk management strategies. The intention is to carry out the program or activity in a way that minimizes the possibility of a problem occurring and/or lessens the severity of any losses that do occur. To mitigate the risks associated with experiment preparation, measures such as providing training and supervision, setting up multiple experiment stations to ensure student participation, and bringing extra equipment could be implemented. With the chosen risk controls or transfers in place, evaluate the risks related to the program or activity.

Based on the risk assessment, decide whether to continue with the program or activity as is or make modifications. Put the chosen risk management strategies into practice and track the outcomes. It is crucial to assign responsibility for putting the chosen risk management measures into action and to establish a deadline for finishing those activities.

The remaining risk is measured using "frequency" and "severity" once the proper risk management strategies have been put into place. If the frequency or likelihood of a loss occurs often or often, then activities or programs that involve duties that pose a high severity of loss such as catastrophic injuries or death, large property damage, or significant operational interruptions should be avoided. Activities that carry a high risk of injury but a moderate or low incidence of injury need to be, at the very least, well monitored and need liability releases from participants.

The majority of the University's programs and activities involve duties that have a moderate risk of loss, such as modest injuries, property damage, or disruptions to operations, as well as a moderate to low frequency of loss. However, these exercises need to be well organized and supervised. There is very little need for risk management in activities or programs that involve a small degree of loss, such as injuries that only need first aid or minor medical attention, little to no property damage, and low chance of loss.

Long-term Vision and Flexibility

The foundation of a company's strategic resilience is the marriage of flexibility and long-term vision. Developing a compelling long-term vision gives teams a feeling of direction and a North Star that shines beyond the present difficulties.

Anticipating changes in consumer tastes, technology improvements, and industry upheavals is an essential component of a strong long-term vision. It fosters an ongoing commitment to innovation and sustainable practices, going beyond short-term rewards. This vision serves as the focal point that brings everyone together and gives the company direction and purpose.

But in a world where things are changing so quickly, adaptability is also crucial. Unexpected hiccups must be managed by businesses, and they must adjust as needed. This necessitates a readiness to modify tactics, accept new technology, and change directions without sacrificing the essential principles embodied in the long-term vision.

Astute leadership is necessary to strike the correct balance between a firm long-term vision and the flexibility to change course. It entails creating an environment in which change is welcomed as a chance for development rather than something to be feared.

CHAPTER 5: Employee Engagement

Employee engagement is the heartbeat of successful organizations in 2024, transcending the conventional view of a workforce to a dynamic community where each member feels valued and integral to the company's success. Central to effective employee engagement is a culture of open communication. Companies are fostering environments where feedback flows freely, creating a two-way street where employees not only receive guidance but actively contribute ideas and insights. This inclusivity not only enhances job satisfaction but also fuels innovation as diverse perspectives come to the forefront.

Recognition and appreciation are pivotal strategies in employee engagement. Beyond traditional performance reviews, businesses are adopting continuous recognition programs that celebrate both individual and team accomplishments. Acknowledging and rewarding effort fosters a positive work environment and cultivates a sense of pride among employees.

Professional development has become synonymous with employee engagement. Businesses are investing in learning and growth opportunities, providing avenues for skill development and career advancement. This not only enhances employee retention but also ensures a skilled and adaptable workforce. Moreover, the emphasis on work-life balance is a crucial facet of employee engagement. a crucial facet of employee engagement.

Companies are recognizing the importance of flexible work schedules, remote options, and mental health support. Striking a balance between professional responsibilities and personal well-being is fundamental to keeping employees motivated and satisfied.

Motivating and Empowering Teams

In 2024, inspiring and enabling teams will require a more sophisticated strategy that goes beyond conventional leadership models. In the modern workplace, when teamwork and flexibility are critical, competent leaders recognize the value of building an inspired and capable group.

Purpose is essential to motivation. Workers look for purpose and a feeling that they are making a difference in the world. Effective leaders create a compelling vision and match specific responsibilities with the overall objectives of the company. Individuals are inspired and a sense of purpose is fostered in the group as a result of the link between individual efforts and the larger mission.

A trusting culture is necessary for team empowerment. Team members must be given liberty and responsibility by their leaders. This fosters a sense of accountability and ownership while also enabling people to demonstrate their abilities. Encouraging teams to take initiative and own initiatives allows them to perform to their best.

Acknowledgment has great motivational power. Recognizing and applauding accomplishments, regardless of size, creates a pleasant work environment. Acknowledgment by the public not only raises spirits but also sets a positive example for others, fostering a culture that values achievements.

For both empowerment and incentive, effective communication is essential. Transparent leaders who set clear expectations and provide constructive criticism create a culture where team members feel informed and involved. Establishing regular avenues of communication, whether through team meetings or individual check-ins, fosters discussion and cooperation.

Possibilities for ongoing education are essential to empowerment. Leaders support their teams' professional development because they understand that learning new skills benefits people as well as the organization as a whole. This focus on education encourages a creative and adaptive culture.

Effective Communication Strategies

Communication skills are essential for a successful profession. Effective communication in the workplace can foster greater collaboration and teamwork, lessen conflict by lowering the likelihood of misunderstandings, and offer emotional support to all team members. Developing your communication skills will help you forge stronger bonds with your coworkers, clients, and staff. In addition to increasing engagement, effective communication can foster creativity and increase team buy-in.

Techniques for effective business communication

You need to be proficient at asking for feedback, delivering messages, and actively listening in order to communicate effectively. These are a few of our most preferred methods for improving communication abilities.

Adapt the message to suit the readership: Learning how to modify your communication (style and messaging) for various audiences is one of the first steps toward effective communication. You can delve deeper into the specifics of implementation because your safety team is likely already aware of the issue if you're discussing a new policy with them. However, modify your messaging when implementing the same guideline for frontline staff members.

You'll probably take a more comprehensive approach. Describe the goal of the policy and the practical implementation that should be done on a daily basis. This holds true in all circumstances. A gathering of kindergarteners, tech entrepreneurs, cattle farmers, and fitness professionals would all respond to you differently depending on the subject matter, the message you want to get across, and the setting of the conversation.

Get ready to deliver the message: What position are you in? Do you have a friendly and open body language? Are you staring at a screen or maintaining a lot of eye contact?

Prepare yourself before engaging in any kind of communication, be it a formal speech or a one-on-one meeting. Before giving a presentation or reviewing the agenda for a meeting, you could take a few minutes to take deep breaths.

Communicate with sincerity: A piece on Quantified Communications claims that real leaders have communications that are 29% clearer and are 50% more impassioned. They radiate openness and warmth. They are completely present in the conversation and have a sense of immediacy when speaking with coworkers and subordinates. Additionally, people desire to collaborate more with real communicators and leaders. In the end, having integrity and dependability makes your work easier since others will want to work with you.

When you speak, show passion and interest: Positive stimuli are received more readily by people. The best ways to communicate more effectively are to smile and express your excitement. You can increase the likelihood that someone will listen to you and believe what you're saying by employing these strategies.

Control nonverbal cues to steer the conversation: Albert Mehrabian, a body language researcher, claims that just 7% of communication is verbal and that the other 38% is vocal. This implies that controlling your nonverbal cues is crucial. Your listeners will assume you aren't interested in the conversation if you are often looking at the clock and pointing your feet in the direction of the door. Your spoken words and nonverbal cues need to match for effective communication. Engage in active listening when others reply to you. Being attentive doesn't only mean hearing what someone has to say. It entails demonstrating your interest in the conversation by posing queries and paying attention to what others have to say. You may strengthen your relationship with someone by showing that you are interested in what they have to say and by being an active listener. It also aids in your memory of specifics spoken in the chat.

Are there folks you know who can never forget a name? Most likely, they actively listen. Repetition of the person's name during an introduction is one strategy. However, you can also do this when working on projects by restating instructions or clarifying what someone has said to make sure you understand them completely. Making eye contact, leaning forward, and nodding are further indicators of engagement.

Request input from your teammates: Asking for feedback is one of the best and most efficient strategies to enhance your communication. Change is ultimately how most of us learn and develop.

Establish a procedure for providing feedback first: This could be conducted in-person or as a quick survey after the meeting. Establish an open-door policy as well to give staff members confidence to come to you with any issues.

Ask to be understood in order to make sure you are being heard: By raising questions, you demonstrate to the speaker your interest in the discussion. It also provides you with more details and an organic way to improve active listening.

Respectfully resolve disputes: It is inevitable that disagreements will arise between coworkers, superiors, and employees. If you want to maintain your professional connection, you must speak respectfully even if you don't agree on everything. Never say anything in rage that you would wish to take back once you've calmed down, as a general rule.

Employ the appropriate equipment: Selecting the appropriate tool can be the best advice for efficient communication at times. Tools like email, Slack, one-on-one talks, team discussions, and group meetings have their proper uses. It is important to consider the advantages and disadvantages of each instrument before selecting one over the other.

- Email: For quick updates and inquiries, people communicate via email. Email can easily get out of control if you need to address a complex topic or want to have a group conversation. Use a separate tool for more complicated matters.

- Slack: Because it allows for both group and individual discussions across several channels, Slack is effective for all kinds of conversations. Because of its integrations with over 2,000 apps, like nTask, Time Doctor, Dropbox, Drift, and Trello, your teams may work concurrently in other tools without having to jump between contexts. You can start a meeting directly in the chat window, send a file in one project channel, and provide prompt feedback in another.

Individual instruction and constructive criticism are two excellent uses of one-on-one interactions. However, they aren't the best option if you need to give a brief update or address issues to a team. For delicate or complicated discussions, have one-on-one discussions.

- Team talks: These are usually quick, spontaneous conversations. Use these for stand-ups and scrums, or for real-time group collaboration with a specific aim in mind. Don't use these for updates on projects where most attendees won't be affected or where there isn't much overlap. Meetings in groups are excellent when you need to instruct or update the whole group at once. Apply these judiciously. Send a brief note if you have something to say that can be done so! If a group gathering is necessary, set a time in advance and make sure your agenda is clear and includes the desired results.

Time is of the essence: You must wait for the appropriate opportunity to address a project update or locate a crucial document. Being aware of the deadlines and crunch periods of your coworkers is one of the best ways to improve communication. Someone else will find it difficult to hear what you have to say while they are dealing with an impending deadline or a difficulty at work. Ascertain the day and platform when team members are most receptive to communication. If they check and respond to messages, for instance, after 4 p.m., plan your chat and have it ready for them when they're ready.

Develop your communication skills: Effective communication is essential whether you want to advance in your career or see your project through to completion without incident. You'll be a more genuine and involved speaker and more productive at work and while collaborating with others if you follow these easy steps.

Professional Development Programs

Professional development programs stand as linchpins for both individual career growth and organizational success. These programs go beyond traditional training, evolving into dynamic initiatives that empower employees, foster innovation, and enhance overall workplace effectiveness.

A cornerstone of effective professional development is personalized learning paths. Recognizing the diverse skills and aspirations of employees, businesses are tailoring programs to individual needs. This not only maximizes the impact of the training but also resonates with employees, driving a sense of investment in their professional journey.

Mentorship programs have become instrumental in guiding career trajectories. By pairing experienced mentors with aspiring professionals, businesses are creating avenues for knowledge transfer, skill development, and invaluable networking opportunities. This not only accelerates the learning curve for employees but also strengthens organizational cohesion.

Continuous learning initiatives are at the forefront of professional development. Companies are leveraging online courses, workshops, and seminars to provide ongoing opportunities for skill enhancement. This commitment to continuous learning not only keeps employees abreast of industry trends but also positions businesses as dynamic, forward-thinking entities.

Furthermore, professional development programs are increasingly incorporating soft skills training. Effective communication, leadership, and adaptability are recognized as essential components of a well-rounded professional. These programs are not just about acquiring technical skills but also honing the interpersonal abilities crucial for success in the modern workplace.

CHAPTER 6: Customer-Centric Approach

Customer centricity, which is placing the needs of your customers at the center of everything you do, is a must if you want your business to succeed. However, what is client centricity exactly, and how is it accomplished? It's the capacity of individuals within a company to comprehend the circumstances, viewpoints, and expectations of its clients. To foster customer pleasure, loyalty, and advocacy, the customer should be at the center of all choices pertaining to the delivery of goods, services, and experiences. You may believe that to be simple. Is it really that easy, though?

Anticipating a customer's needs, desires, and communication preferences is a key component of being customer-centric. and finally doing it correctly. You can generate memorable encounters and enduring client relationships if you can accomplish this.

When it comes to marketing, it's critical to think about how the consumer will benefit from and find advertising and marketing initiatives useful. People, for instance, detest being bothered and interrupted, but if an advertisement is relevant to them, they are more likely to remember it and, in the end, act upon it.

Why Does Customer Centricity Matter For Companies And Brands?

Consider client centricity to be both a strategy and a way of life. In order for the customer, who makes the final decision, to notice it, it must become deeply embedded in the business.

Customers won't purchase from you if they are dissatisfied. Furthermore, a business cannot exist without its clientele.

Consider your usual vendors and the reasons behind them. How do they maintain your loyalty? You wouldn't do business with them if they made it difficult for you to do so.

Rather, they simplify it. They employ the tools you have asked them to use to effectively communicate with you. They might even show you offers for products that precisely catch your eye when you're about to make a purchase. Pretty smart, huh?

What about the people you no longer work with? Most likely, they irritated or disturbed you or failed to make you feel wonderful. Did they mislead you with their marketing or bombard you at the inappropriate times? Perhaps you've noticed social media pop-up advertisements for funeral planning or weight loss and questioned why in the world you were seeing them. According to a study, almost one in three consumers will stop doing business with a brand they adore after just one negative encounter. According to the business, "Experience is everything." Make the correct decision. People who have a positive consumer experience feel valued and heard. It keeps a human factor while maximizing efficiency and reducing friction.

Furthermore, research indicates that 84% of consumers anticipate quality businesses to provide content that entertains, solves problems, and engages them through narrative. Personalization is not only important in today's digital world, but it is also required, and businesses are increasingly based on their dedication to acting in the best interests of their clients. There are many who contend that Amazon is a customer-focused business. Due to its size and global reach, it naturally has the resources and technical staff to carefully analyze the purchasing patterns of its clientele and target the appropriate messages through the channels that they most like. Obstacles And Optimal

Strategies for transforming into a Customer-Centric business

Getting the leadership, marketing, sales, service, support, finance, and other departments on board is the first step. Customer-centric marketing can therefore be accomplished by:

Conscientious targeting: Identifying your most probable clients and locating them across various channels.

Producing marketing collateral for the whole client journey: Individuals will become engrossed in various topics at different stages of the journey and require different types of knowledge. For instance, during the awareness stage, we often want to grab their attention, so advertisements should be entertaining, engaging, and brief; conversely, during the contemplation stage, consumers require information, may wish to compare items, and may even wish to learn more. Starting with the correct data is one thing. However, when you collect more information and link it to the client profile, it becomes more relevant over time and aids in the creation of more individualized ads. However, there is a warning that marketers should be aware of: The world of digital marketing is moving toward less identity, less data, and greater privacy (see, for instance, the EU's General Data Protection Regulation and the removal of third-party cookies from the majority of browsers). Targeting someone effectively demands appropriate automation and optimization configurations, which aren't always achievable on a tight budget or with limited data.

Best Practices Focused on the Customer to Help You Realize Your Goals

Establish a customer-focused culture: Make sure that the customer is the center of attention for every employee, including the CEO and front-line staff. Include it in your vision, mission, and values.

Make your data better: Ensure that your data is of higher quality, consistent, and accessible to all members of the business. Data is frequently misused and underutilized. Employees within the organization won't know how to properly analyze and apply it if it's not a concrete asset. AI, for instance, enables data to be linked automatically to identify people and provide insights that enhance next-best-offer programs and customisation. (But note the warning I mentioned above.)

Gather input from clients: It's critical to pay close attention to what your consumers need and want by asking for, reading, and acting upon their feedback to guide your business. Customers aren't always correct. You'll be able to tell when someone is being petty or worse. However, it is beneficial to pay attention to numerous clients who offer similar criticism – either through words or actions.

Have a long-term perspective: A single transaction is not as valuable as a long-term connection with a consumer. Develop a relationship with your clients so they feel like more than just a name or number. Long-term relationships with them lead to loyalty and retention. You may establish these relationships by keeping in touch with them, making personalized offers, and learning about their preferences.

Understanding Customer Needs

Comprehending the demands of customers will be crucial for organizations to succeed as they go beyond the transactional aspect of business and create long-lasting relationships. This comprehension dives deeply into the nuances of consumer preferences, pain concerns, and goals, going beyond interactions at the surface level.

Active listening is a key component of efficient techniques for understanding client demands. Companies are establishing avenues for receiving direct input from consumers and viewing social media, polls, and customer service exchanges as priceless sources of knowledge. In addition to providing information for product or service improvements, this real-time feedback loop demonstrates to consumers that their ideas are appreciated.

Additionally, companies are using data analytics to identify trends and patterns in consumer behavior. Companies can obtain a sophisticated grasp of individual preferences by examining purchasing histories, online interactions, and demographic data. Personalized consumer experiences are made possible by this data-driven strategy, which increases brand loyalty.

Developing empathy is a human-centric approach to comprehending the requirements of your customers. Employers are pushing staff members to put themselves in the clients' shoes in order to create a culture where empathy and understanding are essential to providing excellent customer service, not just trendy terms. Genuine, enduring connections with clients are built on this emotional bond.

Building Lasting Customer Relationships

For professionals that thrive in sales cycles that are lengthy, building enduring client connections is essential to long-term (and repeat!) business. But how do you find time to create those enduring relationships when your calendar is packed and your to-do list is constantly expanding?

Investing in strengthening your relationships with your clientele will also prove to be a wise decision. As opposed to keeping an existing customer, acquiring new ones can cost you up to 25 times as much. Furthermore, the recommendation business you receive from satisfied (retained) customers is essentially free. For this reason, marketing to your current clientele is frequently more successful than acquiring leads or contacting unidentified groups of people.

Here are some pointers for building a genuine relationship with your customers that will entice them to return.

1. It is important to communicate constantly: Your clients must be aware of the current situation. If you are a loan officer and a mortgage seems like it might not go through, or if you are a real estate agent and the house your client wants is under numerous offers, inform your clients as much as you can, as often as you can, and do it proactively. When a sales process is underway, err on the side of excessive communication. So they won't have to keep looking for you to find out what's going on, reach out and give them an update on what's happening, what their options are, and what you think they should do.

2. Be Honest: Obstacles will occasionally arise. Customers won't always receive their wish. The financing arrangement fails. Not enough credit is scored well enough. Their ideal house has a bid from another party. It turns out that the insurance they want would cost a little more than they anticipated. Life happens, and you should be honest about any difficulties or roadblocks you encounter. Facing the music is preferable to running the risk of worse outcomes by putting off receiving unpleasant news. Regaining your client's confidence is extremely tough and time-consuming after it has been lost.

3. Compassion: Recognize your customers. Consider their needs with empathy and make an effort to understand their point of view. Identify their goals and assist them in achieving them. Make sure you have a system in place to track them and take notes so you will know who they are when your client returns in five years. Naturally, needs change throughout time, but try to avoid starting at zero if at all possible. To better service your clients, you may maintain track of their particular histories and information by investing in a CRM platform.

4. Improve Their Quality of Life: Basically, if you make a difference in someone's life, they will remember you and tell their friends and family about you. Although you are undoubtedly offering a service, you will also leave a lasting impression by serving as a mentor and imparting your industry knowledge. It is important for your clients to know that you are available to answer any questions they may have, even if they are unrelated to the transaction. Creating and distributing educational, pertinent, and helpful content to your client is a good approach to accomplish this.

5. Honor Your Faithful Clientele: Make sure to express gratitude to your consumers when they recommend friends and family or become recurring business. Make sure you're expressing gratitude to your VIPs and not just reaching out to them when you're attempting to close a deal. This can be done with a handwritten message, a nice gift, or even a unique offer.

6. Maintain Communication: The last thing you want is for the relationship to fall apart after the transaction is finished. It's imperative to continue the discourse because of this. But when there's no transaction to talk about, how do you do that? Two approaches:

Remember significant occasions and events (such as their birthday, the anniversary of your last correspondence, or the passage of six months since your last encounter) and follow up with a heartfelt letter, card, or phone call. This is the area in which your CRM will truly pay off. Send them informative and interesting content via email and social media in between those personalized touches. These channels of contact remind them that you provided excellent service and that you remain accessible as a reliable expert to address any queries they may have. Clients are more likely to remember you when they need your services again or when a friend needs you if you engage them with engaging content rather than overt sales pitch.

Building relationships is essential to obtaining recurring business and referrals. By maintaining consistency (but not bothersome!) communication, you will make it simple for your former clients to suggest you. Make sure you're not just sending out sales pitches, but also a range of communications. Do you have any irksome pals who never give anything in return, only take everything? Avoid being such a person's business counterpart. If you provide your customers something of value, they will be loyal to you for a very long time.

Utilizing Feedback for Continuous Improvement

The implementation of proactive feedback usage is critical to the concept of continuous improvement. Feedback is a dynamic tool that companies can use to improve processes, innovate a culture of creativity, and improve their products and services. It is not just a post-script.

Establishing avenues for candid and transparent feedback is essential. Businesses are using anonymous suggestion boxes, town hall meetings, and surveys to create regular feedback loops. This inclusiveness gives workers at all levels the freedom to offer their perspectives and gives a clear picture of the organization's advantages and shortcomings.

The emphasis on providing constructive comments is equally vital. It takes more than merely pointing out problems to provide remedies and emphasize accomplishments. This positive attitude creates an atmosphere where feedback is viewed as a tool for development rather than as a means of criticism.

Customer feedback is a treasure trove of information for enhancement; it is not restricted to internal stakeholders. Businesses are refining their products and services by using client feedback from surveys, social media, and in-person interactions. This customer-focused strategy fosters advocacy and loyalty in addition to increasing satisfaction.

Being responsive is really key to using feedback for ongoing improvement. Businesses are embracing agile approaches, making adjustments quickly in response to input instead of waiting for protracted review rounds. This flexibility guarantees that businesses maintain an advantage in a market where quickness is a differentiator.

CHAPTER 7: Financial Management

Financial management in business refers to the process of managing a company's finances in a way that promotes success and complies with legal requirements. That requires both a high-level strategy and practical implementation on the ground.

Explain Financial Management

Financial management is essentially the process of creating a business plan and then making sure every department follows it. A long-term vision may be created with the help of solid financial management, which also makes it possible for the CFO or VP of finance to present statistics on liquidity, profitability, cash runway, and other topics. Several financial tasks, including accounting, fixed-asset management, revenue recognition, and payment processing, are combined into a financial management system. Through the integration of these essential elements, a financial management system guarantees instantaneous insight into an organization's financial condition and streamlines routine tasks, such as period-end close procedures.

The Financial Management Goals

Building upon these foundations, finance managers support their organizations in a number of ways, such as but not restricted to:

Optimizing profits: Share information on factors that could cause the cost of items supplied to rise, such as growing raw material costs.
Monitoring cash flow and liquidity: Make sure the business has adequate cash on hand to pay its debts.

Guaranteeing adherence: Observe all applicable federal, state, and industry rules.

Creating financial scenarios: These are based on projections that take a broad range of probable outcomes depending on market conditions and the current state of the firm.

Control connections: interacting with boards of directors and investors in an efficient manner.

In the end, it comes down to integrating sound management practices into the organization's financial framework.

Financial Management's Range

Four primary domains are included in financial management:

Organizing: The financial manager forecasts the amount of money the business will require to keep a positive cash flow, allot funds for expansion or the addition of new goods or services, and deal with unforeseen circumstances. They then share this information with other business partners. There are various categories into which planning can be divided, such as capital expenses, labor and expenses, and indirect and operating expenses.

Setting a budget: The company's available money is distributed by the financial management to cover expenses like rent or mortgage payments, payroll, raw materials, employee T&E, and other commitments. Ideally, some will remain to save for unexpected expenses and to finance potential new ventures. Businesses often have a master budget, as well as smaller, more focused papers that address specific topics like cash flow and operations. Master budgets can be fixed or variable.

Comparing Static and Flexible Setting a budget

Static Adaptable: Stays the same even if the presumptions made during planning are significantly altered. Adapts in response to modifications in the presumptions made during the planning phase. While Flexible is as it is called.

Controlling and evaluating risk

Executives in line of business rely on their finance managers to evaluate and implement compensating controls for a range of risks, such as:

Risk of the market

impacts the company's stock performance, reporting, and investments; for public firms, these aspects are also affected. could also be a reflection of industry-specific financial risk, such a pandemic that affects eateries or the transition of retail to a direct-to-consumer business model.

Credit danger

The consequences of, say, late payments from clients, which leave the company unable to pay its debts and could have a negative impact on creditworthiness and valuation—factors that determine an organization's capacity to borrow money at reasonable interest rates.

Risk to liquidity

Teams in charge of finance must monitor cash flow, project cash requirements for the future, and be ready to release working capital when required.

Risk associated with operations

This is a broad category that several financial teams are unfamiliar with. It might address things like the possibility of a cyberattack, whether to get cybersecurity insurance, what preparations are in place for disaster recovery and business continuity, and what crisis management procedures are activated in the event that a senior leader is charged with fraud or other wrongdoing.

Methods

The finance manager establishes guidelines for the secure and accurate processing and distribution of financial data, such as invoices, payments, and reports, by the finance team. These documented procedures also specify who within the company is in charge of making financial decisions and who approves them.

Businesses don't have to start from scratch because a range of organization kinds have policy and procedure templates accessible, like this one for NGOs.

Financial Management's Roles

More practically, planning, forecasting, and expense control are the main focuses of a financial manager's work in the aforementioned domains. Issuing P&L statements, determining which product or service lines have the best profit margins or contribute most to net profitability, keeping the budget in check, projecting the company's future financial performance, and developing scenario plans are all part of the FP&A role. Also crucial is cash flow management. The financial manager is in charge of ensuring that there is adequate cash on hand for regular business expenses, such as paying employees and buying supplies for manufacturing. This entails managing cash flow, or keeping an eye on money as it comes in and goes out of the company.

Financial management comprises cash management as well as revenue recognition, which is the process of reporting the company's revenue in accordance with accepted accounting practices. One of the most important aspects of strategic cash management and conservation is balancing accounts receivable turnover ratios. It could seem easy, but this isn't always the case: Some businesses may require payment from clients months after the service is rendered. When do you declare that money to be "yours" and inform investors that everything is well?

Five Ways to Raise Your Turnover Ratio for Accounts Receivable

- Provide accurate and frequent invoices. Money will not arrive on schedule if invoices are not sent out on time.

- Declare the terms of payment at all times. Policies that you haven't informed your clients about cannot be enforced. Point out any modifications you make.

- Provide a variety of payment options. There are new B2B possibilities available. Have you given a payment gateway any thought?

- Establish follow-up alerts. Don't wait to begin collection processes until after consumers are past due. Reminders should be given proactively but not intrusively.

- Take into account giving cash and advance payments a discount. In the retail industry, cash(less) is king. By encouraging clients to pay in advance rather than using your standard credit terms, you may lower your AR costs.

Analyzing the company's financial performance in relation to its plans and budgets is the final step in maintaining financial controls. The financial manager can accomplish this, for example, by comparing line items on the company's financial statements using financial ratio analysis.

Tactical versus Strategic Financial Management

Financial management processes set forth the tactical guidelines for processing daily transactions, completing the monthly financial close, comparing actual expenditure to budget, and making sure you comply with tax and auditor obligations.

More strategically, finance directors use data to assist line-of-business colleagues in planning future investments, identifying opportunities, and creating robust companies. This is how financial management feeds into critical FP&A (financial planning and analysis) and visioning tasks.

The Value of Sound Financial Management

Three pillars of strong fiscal governance are supported by sound financial management:

Planning: Determining the financial steps that must be taken for the business to meet its short- and long-term objectives. For instance, in order to plan scenarios, leaders must insights into present performance.

Making decisions: Supplying current financial reports and information on pertinent KPIs to assist company executives in selecting the optimal course of action for plan execution. Managing ensuring that every department operates within budget, in line with plan, and contributes to the overall vision. All staff members have visibility into the company's growth and know where it is headed thanks to efficient financial management.

Which Three Financial Management Types Are There?

Three more general categories of financial management can be formed from the aforementioned functions:

Budgeting for capital projects: Relates to figuring out what financial changes must be made in order for the business to meet its short- and long-term objectives.

Capital arrangement: Ascertain the best way to finance operations and/or expansion. Taking on debt may be the best option if interest rates are low. A business may also think about selling shares, real estate, or other assets, or it may decide to approach a private equity firm for investment.

Management of working capital:

Making sure there is enough cash on hand for regular operations, such as paying employees and buying raw materials for production, was covered above.

What Does Financial Management Look Like?

Let's say the CEO of a toothpaste company wants to launch a brand-new item called toothbrushes. She will ask the finance manager to advise where those monies should come from, such as a bank loan, and her staff to estimate the cost of making the toothbrushes. Those monies will be acquired by the finance manager, who will make sure they are distributed as cheaply as possible to the toothbrush manufacturing process. If the sales of the toothbrushes are strong, the finance manager will compile information to assist the management team in determining whether to use the earnings to expand the toothbrush line, launch a mouthwash brand, distribute a dividend to shareholders, or pursue other options. The financial manager will make sure the business has enough cash on hand to pay the new employees who are making the toothbrushes throughout the process. In addition, she will assess if the business is making and spending the same amount of money that she projected when she created the project's budget.

Budgeting and Forecasting

The symbiotic processes of forecasting and budgeting have become essential for firms seeking not only financial stability but also strategic growth in the volatile economic environment of 2024. Forecasting foresees possible obstacles and opportunities to facilitate proactive decision-making, while budgeting acts as the financial roadmap outlining how resources will be distributed.

Carefully planning and matching money allocations to corporate objectives are key components of budgeting. It includes projected revenue, capital expenditures, and operating costs. A thorough awareness of previous performance, present market patterns, and reasonable expectations for the future are necessary for striking the correct balance.

Forecasting gives budgeting a forward-looking viewpoint, which makes it complementary. To forecast future results, historical data and market patterns are analyzed. With this kind of foresight, firms can spot possible financial roadblocks, seize new opportunities, and weather economic storms with resilience.

The accuracy and efficiency of forecasting and budgeting have increased due to the integration of technology, including sophisticated analytics and artificial intelligence. Agile decision-making is made easier by real-time data analysis, which helps companies quickly adjust their plans in response to changing market conditions.

An ongoing process of observation and modification is essential. By periodically reviewing predictions and budgets, firms can adjust their financial strategies to reflect evolving conditions. It is a dynamic tool that changes as the business environment does, not a static document.

Financial Decision-Making in Uncertain Times

Making financial decisions in 2024's uncertain environment will demand a combination of strategic thinking and flexibility. Businesses must adopt a sophisticated strategy in these uncertain times, requiring them to be flexible, quick to adapt, and forward-thinking in their financial plans.

First off, scenario planning is becoming increasingly important to firms. Scenario analysis is imagining several possible futures and creating plans to handle them, as opposed to depending just on one prediction. By taking a proactive stance, organizations can better prepare for both favorable and unfavorable events.

In uncertain financial decision-making, risk management becomes a central role. By recognizing and evaluating risks, both external and internal, firms can put mitigating measures in place. Important elements of this risk-centric strategy include contingency planning, comprehensive insurance coverage, and financial diversification.

Another important aspect is using technology to get real-time financial analytics. Businesses may now continuously monitor financial indicators thanks to advanced analytics and artificial intelligence, which provides the data needed to make well-informed decisions. Because of this real-time visibility, firms are more agile and can quickly adapt to changing conditions.

A crucial component in erratic times is financial flexibility. A financially robust approach must include contingency money for unforeseen issues, negotiate flexible terms with vendors, and maintain liquidity. This adaptability also applies to capital expenditures, as companies are taking a more measured and flexible approach.

To put it simply, making financial decisions in unpredictable times calls for a dynamic and comprehensive viewpoint.

Cost Optimization Strategies

Making financial decisions in 2024's and later years in an uncertain environment will demand a combination of strategic thinking and flexibility. Businesses must adopt a sophisticated strategy in these uncertain times, requiring them to be flexible, quick to adapt, and forward-thinking in their financial plans.

First off, scenario planning is becoming increasingly important to firms. Scenario analysis is imagining several possible futures and creating plans to handle them, as opposed to depending just on one prediction. By taking a proactive stance, organizations can better prepare for both favorable and unfavorable events.

In uncertain financial decision-making, risk management becomes a central role. By recognizing and evaluating risks, both external and internal, firms can put mitigating measures in place. Important elements of this risk-centric strategy include contingency planning, comprehensive insurance coverage, and financial diversification.

Another important aspect is using technology to get real-time financial analytics. Businesses may now continuously monitor financial indicators thanks to advanced analytics and artificial intelligence, which provides the data needed to make well-informed decisions. Because of this real-time visibility, firms are more agile and can quickly adapt to changing conditions.

A crucial component in erratic times is financial flexibility. A financially robust approach must include contingency money for unforeseen issues, negotiate flexible terms with vendors, and maintain liquidity. This adaptability also applies to capital expenditures, as companies are taking a more measured and flexible approach.

To put it simply, making financial decisions in unpredictable times calls for a dynamic and comprehensive viewpoint.

CHAPTER 8: Crisis Management

One of the most important organizational tasks is crisis management. Failure can cause a company to lose money, suffer grave consequences for its stakeholders, or even come to an end. Professionals in public relations play a crucial role in crisis management groups. Therefore, a collection of best practices and insights from our understanding of crisis management would be a highly helpful tool for public relations professionals. It is difficult to summarize what is known about crisis management and public relations' part in that body of knowledge because so many practitioners and scholars from a wide range of fields have published volumes about the subject. Define key concepts as the ideal location to begin this endeavor.

The potential harm a crisis could do to an organization, its stakeholders, and an industry is known as the threat in crisis management. Three interconnected hazards can arise from a crisis:

- Financial loss
- Reputational damage
- Public safety

Certain crises, including product damage and industrial mishaps, can cause injuries or even fatalities. By interfering with business operations, reducing market share or buying intentions, or giving rise to crisis-related lawsuits, crises can result in financial loss. A crisis will somewhat harm an organization's reputation and reflect adversely on it. It is obvious that these three risks are connected. While reputations have a financial impact on firms, injuries or deaths will result in financial and reputational harm.Successful crisis management addresses the dangers one after the other. When there is a crisis, public safety must come first. When public safety is neglected, a crisis's damage gets worse. After addressing public safety, issues about finances and reputation are taken into account. The ultimate goal of crisis management is to either lessen the impact of risks or safeguard a company and its stakeholders against them.

The goal of crisis management is to stop or minimize the harm that a crisis can do to a company and its stakeholders
Study has shown that there are three stages of crisis; pre-crisis, crisis, and post crisis.

Preparation and prevention are the main concerns of the pre-crisis period. The actual phase of crisis response is when management has to react to a crisis. In addition to fulfilling obligations made during the crisis phase, such as providing follow-up information, the post-crisis phase searches for ways to better prepare for the next disaster. This item is structured around the tri-part theory of crisis management.

Communication During Crises

The foundation of stakeholder trust and organizational resilience during crises is effective communication. Businesses are proactively releasing correct information, recognizing the gravity of the situation, and clearly outlining the efforts being taken to address it. Clarity and transparency are crucial.

Timely correspondence is essential. Quick reactions stop false information from spreading and give stakeholders access to the most recent data. Whether speaking to staff members, clients, or members of the public, prompt communication fosters trust in the organization's crisis management skills.

Since empathy acknowledges the crisis's human impact, it is incorporated into communication techniques. Enterprises are demonstrating comprehension and empathy, cultivating a feeling of solidarity among interested parties. This human-centered strategy not only strikes an emotional chord but also reaffirms the organization's dedication to its workforce.

Disseminating information widely is ensured by using different channels of communication. Businesses are broadening their communication tactics to efficiently reach a wide audience by utilizing both traditional and digital media.

Most importantly, feedback loops are set up to get opinions from relevant parties. Businesses can address changing requirements and concerns by actively listening to customers' problems.

This shows that they are responsive, which increases credibility and confidence.

Learning from Past Challenges

The compass that leads organizations through the complexities of the ever changing 2024 landscape is the lessons learned from past mistakes. Thinking back on past failures is a powerful tool for building resilience and progress.

First of all, companies are thoroughly reviewing their previous difficulties in a post-mortem manner. This entails analyzing the underlying reasons, comprehending the chronology of occurrences, and pinpointing opportunities for enhancement. Building strategies against recurrent pitfalls requires this reflective process.

Putting into practice solid backup plans that are informed by past experiences is a common approach. Companies are actively detecting possible hazards and formulating ways to reduce them, making sure they are better equipped to handle unanticipated difficulties.

One important lesson from previous difficulties is adaptability. Organizations are fostering cultures that welcome change and motivate teams to quickly adapt to unforeseen challenges. This flexibility serves as a preventative measure against the unpredictabilities that make up the corporate environment.

Additionally, companies are using technology to efficiently archive and analyze historical data. In order to manage risks proactively, machine learning and data analytics are crucial in spotting patterns, trends, and any red flags.

CHAPTER 9: Regulatory Compliance

In industries where rules and regulations are always changing, managing regulatory compliance is a critical concern for firms. Ensuring compliance is essential to building trust, upholding reputation, and sustaining long-term success in addition to helping businesses stay out of legal hot water.

Above all, it is essential to remain knowledgeable about legislation unique to your sector. Legislative environments are ever-changing, with new laws being added or amended regularly. Companies must take a proactive stance and commit resources to continuous compliance oversight. To keep up with developments, this entails hiring legal counsel, making use of compliance tools, and actively participating in industry forums.

A key element of effective regulatory compliance is the implementation of strong internal policies. This entails creating a framework that may be adjusted for future modifications in addition to creating policies that comply with the laws as they stand. Businesses are embracing compliance more and more, including it into daily operations and decision-making procedures.

Finding and fixing compliance gaps requires routine audits and evaluations. These assessments examine the effectiveness of adopted policies and the real practices inside the company, going beyond a checklist approach. It goes beyond only fulfilling the bare minimum to consistently pursue excellence in compliance standards.

Legal compliance and ethical business practices are entwined. Businesses are realizing how important it is to conduct their operations in accordance with moral principles, not simply because it's required by law but also because it's an essential part of corporate social responsibility. Fair labor procedures, open reporting, and a dedication to environmental sustainability are all necessary for this.

In addition, adopting technology is a calculated step toward guaranteeing regulatory compliance. Automation technologies lower the possibility of human error while also streamlining compliance procedures. Data security measures are part of this technological integration and are essential to many compliance laws.

Staying Informed on Industry Regulations

Keeping up with industry laws is a strategic necessity that determines an enterprise's success and longevity, not just a box to check. The regulatory landscape is dynamic and always changing due to societal changes, market forces, and legislative modifications.

Businesses are taking a proactive, all-encompassing approach to keep up with these changes. This entails creating specialized teams or designating compliance officers in charge of keeping an eye on regulatory changes that are unique to their sector. These people serve as the organization's eyes and ears, constantly monitoring the legal scene for developments that could have an effect on operations.

Another important tactic is to actively participate in forums and associations for the sector. These forums act as centers for exchanging ideas, talking about new rules, and coming to a consensus on the opportunities and problems facing the industry. Making connections with colleagues and industry professionals offers insightful viewpoints that help shape a business's compliance plan.

Consulting with legal specialists on a regular basis is essential. Companies are hiring law firms with industry-specific experience or investing in legal advice. This guarantees a sophisticated comprehension of the subtleties of regulations and the capacity to translate legalese into useful business insights.

Utilizing technology is also showing to be essential for remaining informed. It's becoming commonplace to use compliance management software, subscribe to regulatory update services, and use data analytics for regulatory tracking. These technologies enable firms to quickly adjust by automating the process of monitoring changes and by providing real-time notifications.

Ethical Business Practices

In addition to being morally required, ethical business practices are the cornerstone of respectable and long-lasting companies. Beyond only following the law, ethical issues include a dedication to openness, justice, and social responsibility.

Transparency in corporate operations is first and foremost a basic ethical precept. Businesses are realizing how important it is to communicate openly and honestly with all of their stakeholders, including investors, employees, and customers. In today's discriminating market, trust is a valuable asset that is developed through transparency.

An essential component of moral corporate conduct is treating employees fairly. This entails paying fairly, encouraging inclusion and diversity, and maintaining a secure and encouraging work environment. Employers are spending money on employee well-being initiatives because they understand that a contented and driven workforce is not only morally right but also a valuable resource.

Sustainable environmental practices are becoming more and more important to moral company operations. Businesses are embracing environmentally friendly practices, cutting back on their carbon footprints, and implementing eco-friendly projects. This environmentally conscientious strategy not only fits in with social norms but also establishes companies as accountable environmental stewards.

Taking part in socially conscious projects is another important tactic. Businesses are embracing philanthropy into their business models, sponsoring charity causes, and helping their local communities. These programs show a sincere dedication to improving society, even above and beyond the potential for good PR.

Corporate Social Responsibility

Corporate Social Responsibility (CSR) is more than just a catchphrase for business; it is a basic duty and a chance for companies to make significant contributions to the health of the environment and society. CSR includes social impact, environmental stewardship, and ethical behaviors in addition to profit margins.

One essential element of CSR is environmental sustainability. Businesses are proactively implementing eco-friendly procedures, such as using renewable energy sources and cutting back on waste and carbon emissions. This dedication to environmental responsibility not only satisfies a rising segment of environmentally conscious consumers, but also fulfills an obligation to the world.

Beyond monetary donations, social responsibility is an additional facet of corporate social responsibility. Companies are getting involved in their communities and contributing to social welfare, healthcare, and education initiatives. This engagement is about more than simply charity; it's about creating enduring connections and encouraging good change at the local level.

CSR's ethical foundation consists of ethical business practices. Businesses are realizing how important it is to guide their operations in accordance with moral standards, from fair labor practices to transparent supply chains. Customers' trust is increased, and the company draws in talent who cares about social issues.

Furthermore, as part of their CSR programs, businesses are embracing diversity and inclusion more and more. In addition to being morally required, encouraging diversity in the workplace and making sure all workers have equal opportunity are crucial first steps in building a society that is inclusive and equitable.

1. Clearly define your mission and values: Communicate and explain a mission statement and set of values that represent the company's dedication to social responsibility. Make sure these guidelines are in line with the overarching objectives of improving society and the environment.

2. Incorporate Corporate Social Responsibility into company Strategy: Incorporate corporate social responsibility into the broader company plan. This entails taking into account how corporate actions will affect society and the environment and looking for ways to give back to the community.

3. Involved Parties:

Encourage honest and open communication with all parties involved, including as staff members, clients, vendors, and local communities. Engage people in the processes of decision-making concerning social responsibility programs to guarantee sincerity and conformity with their expectations.

4. Involvement and Empowerment of Employees:

Motivate staff members to take part in social responsibility programs. This could be doing volunteer work, lending a hand with neighborhood initiatives, or engaging in eco-friendly corporate policies. Encourage staff members to advocate for social responsibility inside the company.

5. Partnership with the Community: Work together with the local community to ascertain their priorities and needs. Create programs that specifically address these issues to make sure that efforts to uphold social responsibility have a significant and long-lasting effect.

6. Practices for Environmental Sustainability: Incorporate environmentally friendly methods into regular business activities. This can entail lowering waste, using less energy, and implementing environmentally friendly technology. Communicate these actions openly to demonstrate the company's dedication to sustainability.

7. Observing Ethical Supply Chain Guidelines:

Verify that suppliers follow morally and practically sound business procedures. This entails selecting supply chain partners who share the commitment to social responsibility by doing in-depth reviews of them.

8. Determination and Documentation:

Create key performance indicators (KPIs) to gauge the effect of efforts centered around social responsibility. Report on progress, accomplishments, and difficulties on a regular basis to show responsibility and openness.

9. Ongoing Enhancement: Encourage an environment where social responsibility initiatives are always being improved. Evaluate and reevaluate plans on a regular basis, getting input from stakeholders and modifying plans to meet new demands and obstacles.

10. Inform and Engage Clients: Inform clients about the business's social responsibility programs and include them in the action. Provide goods and services that are ethically and sustainably oriented so that consumers can use their purchasing power to influence favorable social and environmental results. Businesses can exceed societal expectations and leave a lasting good impact on the communities they serve by really adopting these methods.

CONCLUSION

As we get to the end of the "Management Guide for Businesses in 2024," we consider the many ideas and insights that have been weaved across its pages. This manual functions as a compass for executives navigating the shifting terrain of modern business, as we find ourselves at the crossroads of extraordinary potential and hitherto unseen obstacles.

Examining new trends in everything from technology integration to environmental practices helps firms thrive in a time of perpetual change, rather than just adapt. It highlights the critical role that good management plays, stressing the mutually reinforcing nature of long-term vision and flexibility, employee involvement, and a dedication to moral and socially acceptable behavior.

The key role is played by strategic planning, which provides companies with a road map for navigating uncertainty and seizing opportunities. Whether it is embracing technology, encouraging creativity, or adjusting to the demands of remote work, strategic planning is shown to be essential to success and resilience.

Responsible corporate citizenship emphasizes the importance of regulatory compliance, keeping up with industry laws, and ethical business practices. These aren't just legal requirements; they are moral imperatives that support firms' sustainability and credibility in the eyes of customers, staff, and the general public.

As we come to an end, there is a call to action that reverberates through the hallways of every company: welcome change, cultivate an innovative culture, and support moral behavior. It is not enough to simply follow trends; one must also set them, lead with integrity, and make a constructive impact on the world in a world where survival depends on adaptability and business reputations are shaped by societal expectations.

Let this manual serve as a catalyst for change and an inspiration for executives to not only run their companies well in 2024, but also to create a future where companies grow, workers are happy, and communities are prosperous. The path doesn't finish with these statements; rather, it starts with the deliberate choices and deeds of each leader who is dedicated to creating a more superior, ethical, and sustainable corporate environment.

REVIEW PAGE

Dear Reader,

I hope you're doing well while I write this. We would like to take this opportunity to thank you for showing interest in the "Management Guide for Businesses in 2024." Your commitment to remaining up to date and involved in modern business procedures makes your insights extremely important to us.

Your input on this guide's content is extremely valuable to us as we work to give executives insightful and useful advice as they navigate the opportunities and difficulties of the ever-changing business world.

We would be delighted to hear your opinions if you have had a chance to read the guide. Positive or negative, your evaluation will add to the current conversation about successful management, new trends, and 2024 success techniques. Your input enables us to improve our strategy and guarantees that our material is still pertinent and helpful to our viewers.

The following questions can help you focus your review:

- Which sections of the handbook most spoke to you?
- Were there any particular tactics or revelations that you felt were especially sensible or thought-provoking?

- Do you think the guide does a good job of addressing the issues that businesses will face in 2024?

You have the option to make your review as long or short as you choose. We appreciate your time and thoughts, and any input you give will be used to help us shape the content we publish in the future.

We strongly recommend that you take some time to peruse the instructions if you haven't already. We look forward to hearing about your impressions on the guide's content and how it relates to your experiences.

We appreciate you taking a look at what we asked. We really appreciate your input to the continuing discussion about efficient business management and look forward to speaking with you.

Warm regards,

Francis A. Wiles

www.ingramcontent.com/pod-product-compliance
Lightning Source LLC
Chambersburg PA
CBHW060042260726
48658CB00004B/1156